T0158896

Kingdom At Work

21 Day Prayer and Devotional Journal

Written by

Apostle Monique Jackson

authorHOUSE®

AuthorHouse™
1663 Liberty Drive
Bloomington, IN 47403
www.authorhouse.com
Phone: 833-262-8899

© 2022 Apostle Monique Jackson. All rights reserved.

No part of this book may be reproduced, stored in a retrieval system, or transmitted by any means without the written permission of the author.

Published by AuthorHouse 03/21/2022

ISBN: 978-1-6655-5536-4 (sc)
ISBN: 978-1-6655-5537-1 (e)

Print information available on the last page.

Any people depicted in stock imagery provided by Getty Images are models, and such images are being used for illustrative purposes only. Certain stock imagery © Getty Images.

This book is printed on acid-free paper.

Because of the dynamic nature of the Internet, any web addresses or links contained in this book may have changed since publication and may no longer be valid. The views expressed in this work are solely those of the author and do not necessarily reflect the views of the publisher, and the publisher hereby disclaims any responsibility for them.

Holy Bible, New International Version®, NIV® Copyright ©1973, 1978, 1984, 2011 by Biblica, Inc.® Used by permission. All rights reserved worldwide.

Acknowledgments

*I am grateful for my dear friend and mentor
Apostle Patrick J. Brown, Executive Director
of The Renewal Center, Concord NC.
Apostle Brown inspired me to write this
companion journal after a discussion of ideas
related to the ministry Kingdom@Work.*

*I want to thank my work family who have
walked along this road with me as the Holy Spirit
continues to unfold the vision. I am grateful for
the support and understanding each of you display.
Thankyou for your love and prayers! Whew!*
"Min. Artavius Brown"
"Evangelist Shauntae Nunez"
"Missionary Robin Williams"
"Evangelist Rhonda Sanders"
"Missionary Wanda Duncan"
"Deacon Rickey Ford"
"Min. Ricardo Nicholas"
"Missionary Dorothy Rivera"
"Evangelist A. Green"
"I am speaking of what I see inside each of you in the spirit'

*Thank-you Prophet Terance Corpening
Jr., my son whom I love.
I appreciate your encouragement and prayers. Your words
helped to push me forward when my load was heavy.
Keep moving forward and don't look back!*

Carmela E, Head-First Glance, LLC
Thankyou Coach Mel for the seeds of wisdom
and professional development. I am so grateful
for you holding me accountable!

This journal was written with the sole purpose of encouraging and providing inspiration to each person who enters the marketplace daily. We spend an incredible amount of time away from home each day to perform our various roles and responsibilities in the workplace. Kingdom citizens enter the workplace with Christ at the center of their being, each time they step into their place of business. This interactive devotional journal has 21 principles and prayers that you can refer to and expand upon through your own personal entries where space has been provided. There is also a quote included for each of the 21 days in the journal. The goal in mind is for individuals to engage with the daily principles and practical applications using the scriptures provided as a foundation for kingdom leadership. This is a self paced journal that can be used to set the tone for your day or to lift you up when days are challenging. The journal was written from the perspective of kingdom leadership standards. It does not matter if you are a director, supervisor, team member, or hourly employee. We are all on the same team in the kingdom and God has a plan and purpose for each of our lives. I hope you will find this devotional journal to be a source of encouragement and strength which adds to your daily routine@work! Remember, the kingdom is within YOU!

Love and Prayers,
Apostle Monique

Genesis 5:1 "When God created mankind, he made them in the likeness of God. He created them male and female and blessed them. He named them mankind."

Day 1- "I have been created to function in greatness @work!"

_____
_____
_____
_____
_____
_____
_____
_____
_____
_____
_____
_____
_____
_____
_____

Prayer: Lord help me to live in your purpose. You created me to thrive and to fulfill my assignment in the earth. Through me others will see your goodness and give you praise!

_____

_____

_____

_____

_____

_____

_____

_____

_____

_____

_____

_____

_____

_____

_____

_____

_____

_____

_____

_____

_____

Colossians 3:23 "Whatever you do, work
at it with all your heart, as working for
the Lord, not for human masters"

*Day 2- "I must do my very best @work. It is important
to work as though employed by the Lord himself. I am
Christ's representation in the earth realm."*

_____
_____
_____
_____
_____
_____
_____
_____
_____
_____
_____
_____
_____
_____
_____
_____
_____
_____
_____
_____
_____

Prayer: Lord please let your light shine through me each day as I perform my duties. Help me to represent your character in my words, actions and deeds. In this way others will see you and my life will bring you glory.

_____
_____
_____
_____
_____
_____
_____
_____
_____
_____
_____
_____
_____
_____
_____
_____
_____
_____
_____
_____

Psalm 55:22 "Cast your cares on the Lord and He will sustain you; He will never let the righteous be shaken."

Day 3- "Do not worry@work. God surrounds me with His love and care. He will keep me safe in the midst of life's storms."

_____

_____

_____

_____

_____

_____

_____

_____

_____

_____

_____

_____

_____

_____

_____

_____

_____

_____

_____

_____

_____

Prayer: Lord, you know all about my concerns in this life. I can rest knowing that you will take care of me and meet all of my needs. I only have to trust in who you are. In the name of Jesus I pray. Amen!

_____

_____

_____

_____

_____

_____

_____

_____

_____

_____

_____

_____

_____

_____

_____

_____

_____

_____

_____

_____

Isaiah 41:10 "So do not fear, for I am with you; do not be dismayed, for I am your God. I will strengthen you and help you. I will uphold you with my righteous right hand."

Day 4- "Do not be afraid@work! The Lord our God is with us. Even when it seems all hope is lost, the Father is with us. He will give you strength in the midst of every trial."

_____
_____
_____
_____
_____
_____
_____
_____
_____
_____
_____
_____
_____
_____
_____
_____
_____
_____

Prayer: Lord God I thank you for never leaving me and providing your strength when I need it most. I am so grateful for your love and care toward me. I do not have to fear because you are with me.

_____

_____

_____

_____

_____

_____

_____

_____

_____

_____

_____

_____

_____

_____

_____

_____

_____

_____

_____

_____

Proverbs 3:5,6 "Trust in the Lord with all your heart and lean not on your own understanding; in all your ways submit to Him, and He will make your paths straight."

Day 5- "Trust in the Lord for every area of your life; even @work. He will never lead you astray. Consult Him before you make decisions and He will be your guide."

_____
_____
_____
_____
_____
_____
_____
_____
_____
_____
_____
_____
_____

Prayer: Lord help me to seek your face before making decisions for my life. I need your guidance and direction every step of the way. Help me to trust your will for my life and I will be successful in all of your ways. In the mighty name of Jesus! Amen!

_____

_____

_____

_____

_____

_____

_____

_____

_____

_____

_____

_____

_____

_____

_____

_____

_____

_____

_____

_____

Psalm 9:1 "I will give thanks to you Lord, with all my heart; I will tell of all your wonderful deeds."

Day 6- "Set the tone for your day@work by giving God thanks through praises. Give God the highest praise! Shout hallelujah to the Lord for He is good and worthy of all praise!"

_____

_____

_____

_____

_____

_____

_____

_____

_____

_____

_____

_____

_____

_____

_____

_____

_____

_____

_____

_____

Prayer: Lord, I lift up my voice and give you praise for this brand new day. I am grateful for your grace and mercy toward me. Help me to never forget your unfailing love. You allow me to see new mercies every day and Lord I am grateful.

_____

_____

_____

_____

_____

_____

_____

_____

_____

_____

_____

_____

_____

_____

_____

_____

_____

_____

_____

Jeremiah 29:11 "For I know the plans I have for you, declares the Lord, plans to prosper you and not to harm you, plans to give you a hope and a future."

Day 7- "God has a plan for my life. He wants to see me succeed and be prosperous. I don't plan to fail. I fail when I do not set goals and create a plan for my life."

_____

_____

_____

_____

_____

_____

_____

_____

_____

_____

_____

_____

_____

_____

_____

_____

_____

_____

_____

Prayer: Lord I am so thankful that you created me as a unique design with purpose instilled within my soul. You made a plan for creation to succeed in all your ways. Your plans for my life will result in fruitfulness.

_____

_____

_____

_____

_____

_____

_____

_____

_____

_____

_____

_____

_____

_____

_____

_____

_____

_____

_____

_____

I Peter 5:6,7 "Humble yourselves,
therefore under God's mighty hand, that
he may lift you up in due time."

*Day 8- "As a kingdom leader I must walk in humility
before God and be an example for those whom I serve @
work."*

_____

_____

_____

_____

_____

_____

_____

_____

_____

_____

_____

_____

_____

_____

_____

_____

_____

_____

_____

Prayer: Lord help us as kingdom leaders to walk in your humility and grace. Teach us how to lead others and be a worthy example which reflects your character.

_____

_____

_____

_____

_____

_____

_____

_____

_____

_____

_____

_____

_____

_____

_____

_____

_____

_____

_____

_____

_____

Titus 2:7 "In everything, set them an
example by doing what is good."

*Day 9- "Lead by example by doing good in all your
ways@work."*

_____

_____

_____

_____

_____

_____

_____

_____

_____

_____

_____

_____

_____

_____

_____

_____

_____

_____

_____

_____

Prayer: Lord teach me your ways. Help me to live a life worthy of the calling in my life.

_____
_____
_____
_____
_____
_____
_____
_____
_____
_____
_____
_____
_____
_____
_____
_____
_____
_____
_____
_____
_____
_____

Proverbs 16:3 "Commit your work to the
Lord and then your plans will succeed."

*Day 10- "Place your work in the hands of the master
and you will enjoy success @work!"*

_____

_____

_____

_____

_____

_____

_____

_____

_____

_____

_____

_____

_____

_____

_____

_____

_____

_____

_____

_____

_____

Prayer: Lord help me to seek your counsel and place my trust in you for my plans. By faith I can depend on you to lead and guide me as I walk out my God given purpose.

_____

_____

_____

_____

_____

_____

_____

_____

_____

_____

_____

_____

_____

_____

_____

_____

_____

_____

_____

_____

_____

_____

I Corinthians 15:58 Therefore my beloved
brothers, be steadfast, immovable, always
abounding in the work of the Lord, knowing
that in the Lord your labor is not in vain."

*Day 11- "Be faithful over the things God has entrusted
to your hands@work."*

_____

_____

_____

_____

_____

_____

_____

_____

_____

_____

_____

_____

_____

_____

_____

_____

_____

_____

_____

Prayer: Lord help me to be faithful over the things you have entrusted to me. Give me the strength and grace to fulfill the assignment.

_____

_____

_____

_____

_____

_____

_____

_____

_____

_____

_____

_____

_____

_____

_____

_____

_____

_____

_____

_____

_____

Proverbs 14:23 "All hard work brings a profit,
but mere talk leads only to poverty."

*Day 12- "God desires that we keep our commitments@
work and follow through on the work assigned to us."*

_____

_____

_____

_____

_____

_____

_____

_____

_____

_____

_____

_____

_____

_____

_____

_____

_____

_____

_____

_____

_____

_____

Prayer: Lord give me the grace to keep my word@work. It's not enough to say what I will do but instead to complete the task at hand. Teach me to manage my time accordingly and to have balance in my life.

_____

_____

_____

_____

_____

_____

_____

_____

_____

_____

_____

_____

_____

_____

_____

_____

_____

_____

_____

_____

James 1:5 "If any of you lacks wisdom, you should ask God, who gives generously to all without finding fault, and it shall be given to you."

Day 13- *"Ask the Lord for wisdom as a kingdom leader@work. You will make sound decisions when God's wisdom is applied in every area of our lives."*

_____
_____
_____
_____
_____
_____
_____
_____
_____
_____
_____
_____
_____
_____
_____
_____
_____
_____

Prayer: Lord you said in your word that I can ask for wisdom and that you would provide. I need your guidance in all of my ways. Please give me the grace to accept your will for my life. In Jesus name. Amen!

_____
_____
_____
_____
_____
_____
_____
_____
_____
_____
_____
_____
_____
_____
_____
_____
_____
_____
_____
_____

Isaiah 40:30 "But those who hope in the Lord will renew their strength. They will soar on wings of eagles; they will run and not grow weary, they will walk and not be faint."

Day 14- *"The Lord gives strength to the weary@work! He will give you grace to make the journey! Hold on!"*

_____

_____

_____

_____

_____

_____

_____

_____

_____

_____

_____

_____

_____

_____

_____

_____

_____

_____

Prayer: Lord I can't make it without you! I need your reassurance and strength to fulfill my calling and mission in the earth. You are my source of strength and power. I need you every moment of the day.

_____

_____

_____

_____

_____

_____

_____

_____

_____

_____

_____

_____

_____

_____

_____

_____

_____

_____

_____

Romans 15:13-"May the God of hope fill you with all joy and peace as you trust in him, so that you may overflow with hope by the power of the Holy Spirit."

Day 16- "God will give you joy and peace during the course of your day@work. When we think on His goodness the result is a grateful heart"

_____

_____

_____

_____

_____

_____

_____

_____

_____

_____

_____

_____

_____

_____

_____

_____

_____

_____

_____

_____

_____

Prayer- Lord help me not to focus on the challenges I may experience at work. Instead help me to place my trust in you and find peace in the midst of struggles. You are a waymaker and I will come out of this stronger than before! Amen!

_____

_____

_____

_____

_____

_____

_____

_____

_____

_____

_____

_____

_____

_____

_____

_____

_____

_____

_____

_____

_____

James 1:2 "Consider it pure joy my brothers and sisters whenever you face trials of many kinds, because you know that the testing of your faith develops perseverance."

Day 17- "Our faith is cultivated when we are faced with periods of testing@work."

_____

_____

_____

_____

_____

_____

_____

_____

_____

_____

_____

_____

_____

_____

_____

_____

_____

_____

_____

_____

Prayer: Lord help me to go about my daily routine with joy and a grateful heart. I am excited to perform my day to day assignments. Bless me to display a positive attitude in the workplace even when I am being tested.

_____

_____

_____

_____

_____

_____

_____

_____

_____

_____

_____

_____

_____

_____

_____

_____

_____

_____

_____

_____

Psalm 37:4 "Take delight in the Lord and He will give you the desires of your heart."

Day 18- "The Lord wants us to work; but He also wants us to have joy while we are serving@work."

_____
_____
_____
_____
_____
_____
_____
_____
_____
_____
_____
_____
_____
_____
_____
_____
_____
_____
_____
_____
_____

Prayer: Lord help me to have a grateful heart while I am serving others at work. Help me to delight myself in you by serving and being an example of a kingdom leader.

_____

_____

_____

_____

_____

_____

_____

_____

_____

_____

_____

_____

_____

_____

_____

_____

_____

_____

_____

_____

Genesis 2:2 "By the seventh day God had finished the work he had been doing; so on the seventh day he rested from all his work."

Day 19- If God took time to rest after creating so should we. He took time to admire and reflect on his wonderful creation. Take time to pause and reflect during the workday. It is necessary@work!

_____

_____

_____

_____

_____

_____

_____

_____

_____

_____

_____

_____

_____

Prayer: Lord help me to be faithful while I am performing my daily tasks at work. Lead me to live a balanced life by incorporating devotional time with you and rest for my physical body.

_____

_____

_____

_____

_____

_____

_____

_____

_____

_____

_____

_____

_____

_____

_____

_____

_____

_____

_____

_____

Psalm 32:8 "I will instruct you and teach you in the way you should go: I will counsel you with my loving eye on you."

Day 20- The Lord provides instruction and wise counsel to those who place their trust in Him@work.

_____
_____
_____
_____
_____
_____
_____
_____
_____
_____
_____
_____
_____
_____
_____
_____
_____
_____
_____
_____

Lord, please help me to look to you for instruction and guidance throughout my day. I can lay my concerns at your feet and you will provide wise counsel. In Jesus' name we pray. Amen!

_____

_____

_____

_____

_____

_____

_____

_____

_____

_____

_____

_____

_____

_____

_____

_____

_____

_____

_____

_____

Isaiah 26:3 "You will keep in perfect peace those whose minds are steadfast, because they trust in you."

Day 21- We must keep our minds focused on Christ in order to maintain perfect peace. We each have busy days @work that can at times be fast paced and require mental agility.

_____
_____
_____
_____
_____
_____
_____
_____
_____
_____
_____
_____
_____
_____
_____
_____
_____
_____
_____

Prayer: Lord help me to remain in your peace by meditating on your word daily. When my days become stressful and packed with tasks to perform, help me to remember whose I am and why you created me.

_____

_____

_____

_____

_____

_____

_____

_____

_____

_____

_____

_____

_____

_____

_____

_____

_____

_____

_____

_____

_____

Kingdom @ Work

Our 5 Tenets:

- Connecting to Christ@Work
- Creating Community@Work
- Cultivating Faith@Work
- Creating a Caring Culture@Work
- Character Development@Work

Visit Our Website

Kingdomwrk.com

Printed in the United States
by Baker & Taylor Publisher Services